VLAD

– AND THE –
FIRST WORLD WAR

WRITTEN BY KATE CUNNINGHAM

ILLUSTRATED BY SAM CUNNINGHAM

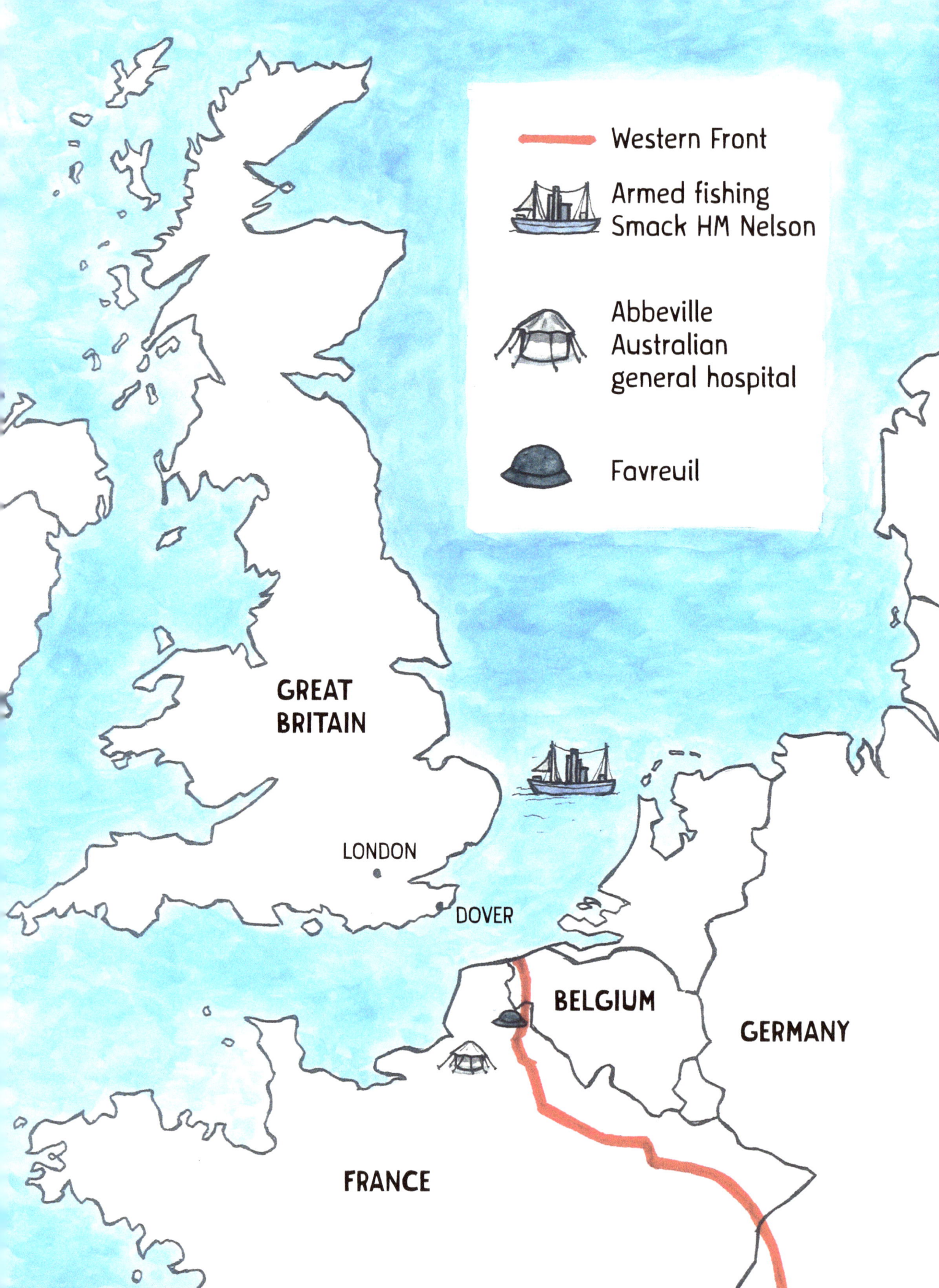

One hundred years ago, soldiers (including Vlad) often used words that are hard to understand now. Here are some explanations.

Artillery very large, powerful guns which moved on wheels. Also the section of the army trained to use these guns.

Biplane an aeroplane with 2 pairs of wings, one above the other.

Blighty Britain.

Chats lice: Small insects that live on animals, including humans, and bite them.

Dog fight a fight in the air between 2 enemy aeroplanes.

Enemy at 6 o'clock a way to explain where the enemy is; "6 o'clock" means the enemy is behind you.

Howitzers a type of artillery.

No-man's-land the ground between the German and Allied trenches which did not belong to either side.

Occupied Belgium the part of Belgium that had been invaded by the Germans.

Our boys what British people called our soldiers.

Over the top climbing out of the trench to attack the enemy.

Shell explosive fired out of artillery weapons.

Smack fishing boat.

Squab baby pigeon.

Stretcher bearers people who carry injured soldiers to the first aid tents.

Torpedo underwater missile.

Trench a deep ditch dug into the ground, where soldiers could move around out of sight of the enemy.

Triplane an aeroplane with 3 pairs of wings, each one above the other.

U-boat German submarine.

VC Victoria Cross: The highest award for bravery.

Vee gheluk good luck in Flemish (spoken in Belgium).

Western Front the area where the armies met and fought in Europe.

White cliffs of Dover cliffs along the south east coast of England facing France. They look white because the rock is chalk.

I'm Vlad the flea, and this is my friend Crisp VC, the carrier pigeon. Look at him, sleeping like a squab. He's recovering from our latest perilous mission.

Crisp VC is a war hero. So am I of course, but I prefer to keep it quiet. The soldiers don't really like me, which is surprising as they are very close to my cousins, the chats. They even share their uniforms.

It's been three years since Crisp VC got his name, after saving our comrades' lives.

We were on an armed fishing boat, a smack called the Nelson. Suddenly we saw a German U-boat rising from beneath the water. The crew aimed their guns, but the submarine had already fired a torpedo which smashed into the side of our vessel.

The skipper, Thomas Crisp, was mortally wounded and the ship was sinking.

Despite his terrible injuries, Thomas wrote a message explaining where we were. Attaching it to my friend's leg he released us and we flew to fetch help. Because of this note all the crew were found and rescued . . . except Thomas who was awarded the Victoria Cross for his brave action. Since that day my friend has been called Crisp VC in his memory.

After our sea adventures we thought it might be drier and safer in France. Well it wasn't! Racing with reports between the trenches and the command centre, we had to fly faster than bullets and be swifter than shells.

But we were **not** just ordinary messengers.

Can you keep a secret? What I am about to tell you is very hush-hush.

We are British spies.

Last week we literally dropped behind enemy lines. Our mission was in occupied Belgium.

We would be collecting coded information which could help win the war. Whilst we waited to return to Blighty the noise of the howitzers became even louder. A huge battle was starting, and we were about to fly right into it.

As dawn broke, the secret agent attached the note to Crisp VC's leg. "Vee gheluk, get safely to England." he whispered as he sent us on our way.

The sun was still coming up as we swooped and soared over German soldiers marching forward to join the fighting.

We reached the trenches just as the artillery stopped firing. There was no noise except the song of the skylarks singing. Even the birds were fighting over every bit of muddy ground. From high in the sky we looked down on the enemy silently advancing over no-man's-land, covered by fog. The low clouds muffled their footsteps and hid them from our boys.

Below I could see Second Lieutenant Walter Tull in his trench, encouraging his men and preparing them to go over the top. I recognised him from the Footballer's Battalion formed right at the start of the war.

"Hey, Walter. Watch out they're coming." I yelled.

He seemed to be shouting back at us, pointing and waving; we pulled higher and seconds later I heard the noise of an aircraft.

Quickly I turned to see the danger.

The safest place would be high above the shooting and away from the imminent dog fight. But the British pilot hadn't seen the Red Baron on his tail, and Crisp VC was not going to leave a fellow flier in danger.

Crisp dived steeply. Coming in behind our pilot he slowed and flapped frantically. The commotion caused the aviator to turn in time to see the red triplane closing in on him.

Banking sharply to the left he avoided the hail of bullets zipping in from the rear.

We flew up and out of range. We had done all we could to help and now we needed to get our message back.

As we swooped over the reserve trenches they seemed very close and I realised Crisp VC was getting lower.

"You need to pull up." I called desperately.

It was then I realised that Crisp VC had been hit by one of the bullets and his wing was bleeding. My friend was struggling to stay in the air, but was getting weaker with every beat of his wings.

Below us were stretcher bearers from the Chinese Workers Corps carrying casualties to a medical tent. Nurses and doctors waited to start treating the injured. I directed my friend down onto a wounded soldier.

We were lifted gently off our passenger.

"Dr Chapple, there's a pigeon with a message."

"He could be vitally important. We need to get him back in action."

The doctor pulled out his wing, bathing it and pressing on the wound to stop the bleeding. With a drink of water and some crumbs to eat, Crisp VC gradually revived and staggered to his feet.

Then he straightened up, ruffled his feathers, stretched his neck and took to the air. We circled once and Crisp VC tipped his wings to the staff who had helped him back on his way.

We had reached the coast and were about to say goodbye to France. Other soldiers were leaving too.

The Indian Cavalry Division were preparing their horses to embark for the Middle Eastern Front in Egypt.

Soon we were struggling against the gusts of wind and crashing waves of the English Channel. We flew over boats packed with new troops on their way to war. Finally, we could see the white cliffs of Dover. They had never looked so beautiful . . .

The handlers rushed Crisp off to be treated and to send our special message through to Headquarters.

We're ready to go again. It's been nearly four years since this noise and fighting began. Do you think it will ever be quiet again, Crisp?

THE PEOPLE

Skipper Thomas Crisp was one of many fishermen working in dangerous conditions to ensure food for Britain during the war. Fishing crews also watched and defended against German U-boats. Thomas Crisp was awarded a posthumous Victoria Cross and the pigeon that took the message was called Crisp VC after him.

Second Lieutenant Walter Tull was a footballer for Tottenham Hotspur before the war. In 1914 footballers joined together to form the Footballer's Battalion. Walter trained as an officer in 1917. On 25th March 1918 he lead his men into battle at Favreuil where he died.

Dr Phoebe Chapple was an Australian medic who paid for her own ticket to travel to Britain where she joined the Women's Auxiliary Army Corps. She was sent to France and received the Military Medal for treating injured staff when their shelter was bombed.

Captain Manfred von Richthofen, the Red Baron, was a German pilot. He shot down over 100 aircraft before being brought down himself on 21st April 1918. He was successful because of his skilful flying, fast plane and his tactic of stalking his enemy.

FACT FILE

World War One started in August 1914 and ended on 11th November 1918. It is sometimes known as the Great War, because people hoped it would be the last war to be fought by so many countries.

NUMBER FACTS

- 32 countries were involved.
- 65 million people participated in some way.
- 8.7 million served Britain.
  - 5.7 million of these soldiers were from the United Kingdom.
  - 3 million of them were from Canada, Australia, New Zealand, Southern Africa, India, Pakistan, Bangladesh, Burma and the Caribbean.
- 140,000 Chinese men travelled to Europe. They did not fight but dug trenches, built train tracks and carried loads.
- 100,000 pigeons flew vital messages all around the battlefields through great danger. They were a successful and reliable way to pass messages and saved many thousands of human lives during the war.

The pigeons were donated by pigeon fanciers in Britain to support the Allied war effort. They did not charge for this gift to the country and bred and trained them to act as carriers so they were ready for action.

ALSO IN THE SERIES

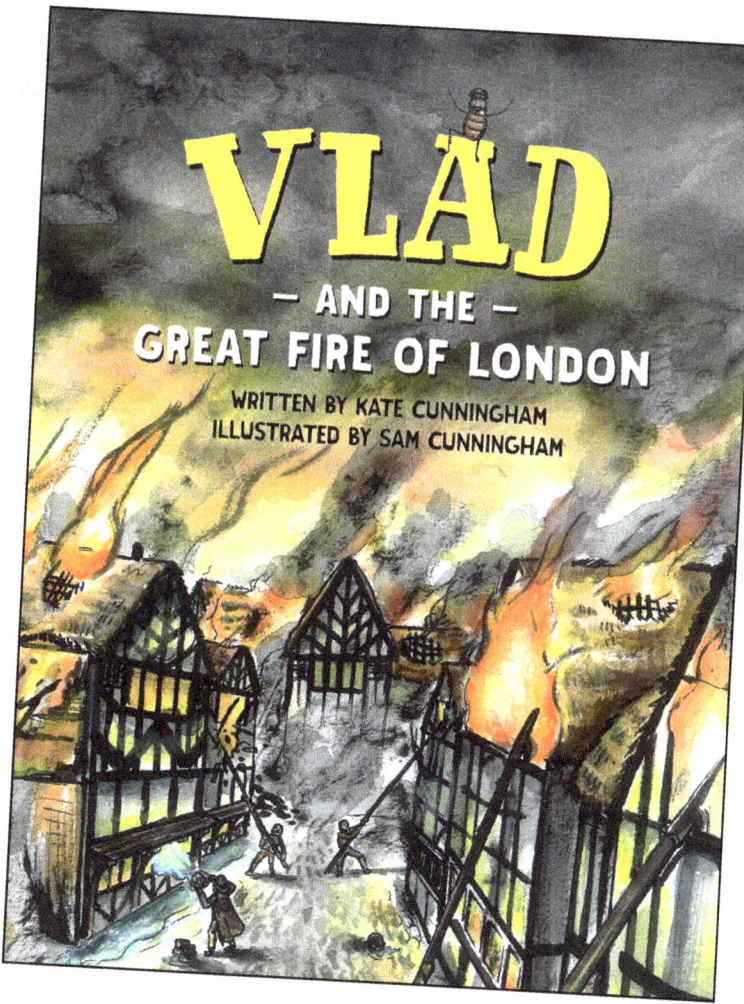

It is 1666 and Vlad the flea and his friend Boxton the rat, love eating and biting their way around London.

But one night in Pudding Lane they are caught up in a fire that threatens to destroy them, along with most of the City of London.

A classroom essential – An innovative, multi-faceted resource which brings the reality of London in 1666 to life in a thoroughly engaging manner!
F. Suleman, Assistant Head Teacher

This is how big Vlad really is

For Sean, our resident expert historian.

Thanks are due to Danny, Freddie and Sue
for listening and reading over and over again!
Any errors are the responsibility of the author.

VLAD AND THE FIRST WORLD WAR

Written by Kate Cunningham
Illustrated by Sam Cunningham

This paperback edition published 2017 by Reading Riddle

This edition designed by Rachel Lawston, lawstondesign.com

ISBN: 978-0-9955205-2-3

Text copyright © Kate Cunningham
Illustrations copyright © Sam Cunningham

The right of Kate and Sam Cunningham to be identified as the
Author and Illustrator of this work has been asserted by them in
accordance with the Copyright Designs and Patents Act 1988.

All rights reserved.

www.ingramcontent.com/pod-product-compliance
Lightning Source LLC
Chambersburg PA
CBHW061932290426
44113CB00024B/2888